SATCHEL PAIGE
DON'T LOOK BACK

Written by
DAVID A. ADLER

Illustrated by
TERRY WIDENER

HARCOURT, INC.   Orlando   Austin   New York   San Diego   Toronto   London

www.HarcourtBooks.com

Library of Congress Cataloging-in-Publication Data
Adler, David A.
Satchel Paige: don't look back/written by David A. Adler; illustrated by Terry Widener.
p.   cm.
Includes bibliographical references.
1. Paige, Satchel, 1906–1982—Juvenile literature.   2. Baseball players—
United States—Biography—Juvenile literature.   3. Discrimination in sports—United States—
History—Juvenile literature.   I. Widener, Terry, ill.   II. Title.
GV865.P3A34   2007
796.357092—dc22   2005026354
ISBN-13: 978-0-15-205585-1 ISBN-10: 0-15-205585-1

First edition
A C E G H F D B

Manufactured in China

The illustrations in this book were done in Golden acrylics on Strathmore bristol board.
The display type was set in Ivy League.
The text type was set in Sheriff.
Color separations by Bright Arts Ltd., Hong Kong
Manufactured by South China Printing Company, Ltd., China
This book was printed on totally chlorine-free Stora Enso Matte paper.
Production supervision by Jane Van Gelder
Designed by Linda Lockowitz

For Itzi and Irene

—D. A. A.

To Frank M., a great baseball fan

—T. W.

> **"**Only one person
> can pitch like me. I could
> nip frosting off a cake
> with my fast ball.**"**

Satchel Paige may have been the best pitcher ever. He pitched thousands of games during a lifetime in baseball. And he won most of them. For most of his career, though, he was kept out of the "big show," the major leagues. Until the late 1940s, the major leagues were for whites only—Paige was an African American.

Leroy "Satchel" Paige was born in Mobile, Alabama, the seventh of eleven children of Lula and John Paige.

His mother was a cleaning woman, and his father a gardener.

For many years Paige let reporters and fans guess about his age.

The mystery was fun and good publicity. Later, Paige explained it by saying, "Age is a question of mind over matter. If you don't mind, it don't matter."

Once his playing days were done, he admitted to having been born on July 7, 1906.

The Paige family was poor, so when Leroy was seven, he found work at the train depot. He rigged up a pole and some rope to carry several bags and satchels at once for busy travelers. Some said he looked like "a walking satchel tree." From then on he was known as Satchel Paige.

Paige also worked sweeping up at a local baseball field. He watched games there and got interested in playing. He didn't own a baseball, so he practiced by throwing rocks. He had a real talent for it.

When he was ten, he joined his school's team. At first he played in the outfield, but the coach saw how well he could throw a baseball. Soon he was the team's top pitcher.

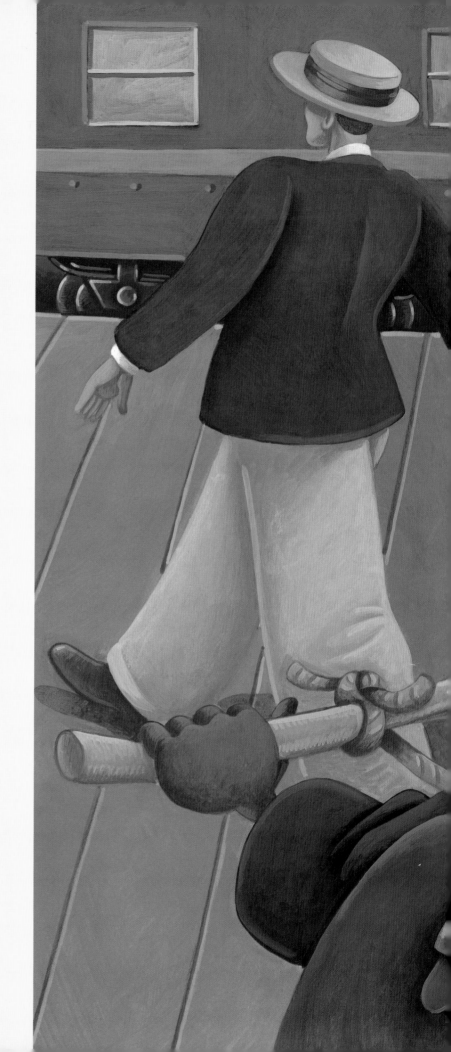

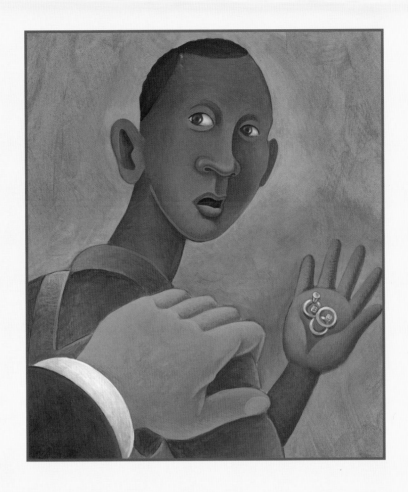

Paige didn't like to study or go to class, but he loved to play baseball. The only time he was sure to be in school was when there was a game. Otherwise, he spent time in the streets with his friends— and sometimes they got into trouble. When Paige was twelve, he was arrested for stealing a handful of rings from a toy store and sent to a reform school in Mount Meigs, Alabama.

Paige was never bitter about spending more than five years in reform school. "When you grow up as poor as me," he said, "a place like Mount Meigs can be mighty warm and good."

He played baseball there and impressed the coach, who told him, "That arm may do you some good some day."

The coach was right.

Paige was seventeen when he got out of Mount Meigs, and he needed to work. He went to the manager of the local semiprofessional black baseball team, the Mobile Tigers. Paige showed him how well he played, and he got a job pitching.

No one else pitched like Satchel Paige. He looked to the side, cranked his arms several times, leaned all the way back, kicked his large left foot high up, and then threw the ball. He invented his own pitches: the blooper, looper, drooper, hesitation pitch, wobbly ball, trouble ball, nothing ball, and a whipsey-dipsey-do. His favorite was the "bee" ball, which buzzed like a bee past the batter.

Paige loved the game and wanted to play in the major leagues—but no team would take him because he was black. So instead he played with other great African American ballplayers in the Negro Baseball Leagues. He bounced from teams in Alabama to North Dakota, Cuba, Mexico, and elsewhere, always playing for the team that paid him the most.

And wherever he played, African American fans gathered by the thousands to watch the great Satchel Paige. He once said that if the all-white Yankees and Phillies were in one Philadelphia stadium and he were in another, *he* would draw a bigger crowd.

"You got to understand," said Connie Johnson, a pitcher in the Negro Leagues and later in the major leagues. "He was like Babe Ruth to us, but he was *our* Babe Ruth."

Each fall, after the baseball season ended, all-white major-league all-star teams were formed. Those teams played against local semiprofessional teams, both black and white. Paige pitched on the local teams, sometimes to the greatest white baseball players of his generation. *They* knew how good he was.

Joe DiMaggio called Paige "the best and fastest pitcher I've ever faced."

Ted Williams said, "Satch was the greatest pitcher in baseball."

In the mid-1930s, Dizzy Dean was the best pitcher in the majors. He told Paige, "You're a better pitcher than I ever hope to be."

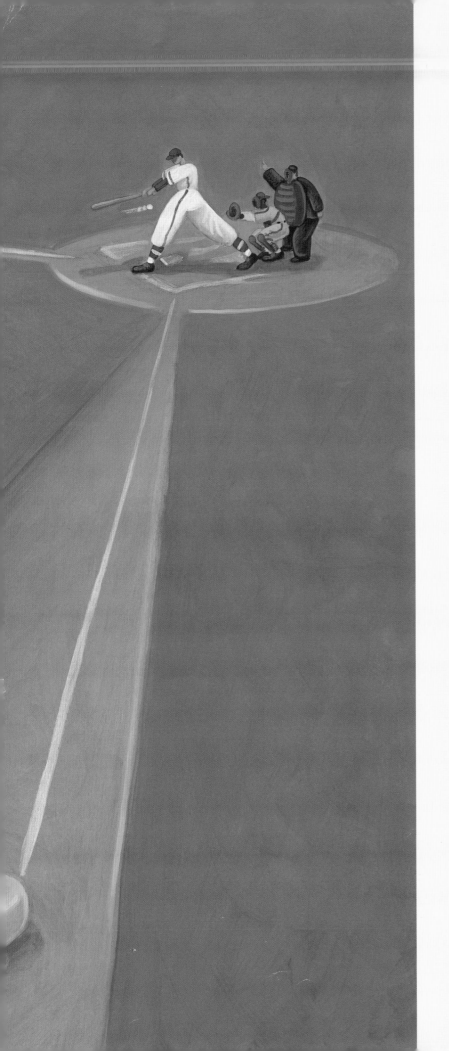

Paige's talent didn't shield him from racism on the field. Players on an all-white semiprofessional team once called him overrated and made racial remarks about him. Paige was furious. He knew it was only bigotry that kept him out of major-league baseball. So he decided he would teach those players a lesson—by beating their team all by himself.

Paige had his teammates sit down on the field and then threw nine strikes in a row—three straight strikeouts!

The white players apologized.

Paige wasn't a bitter man, but he knew he was being cheated. Most newspapers didn't report on his games. Many white baseball fans didn't know his name.

Paige wasn't afraid to speak out. In a 1942 newspaper report he reminded people that baseball fields weren't the only places closed to him and other African Americans. At the time there were also schools, parks, hotels, and jobs closed to blacks. Even if he were able to play with whites, Paige complained, he "still couldn't stay or eat with them in many places."

Throughout much of Paige's career, there was talk of change, of opening the major leagues to people of all races. But it wasn't until 1947 that Jackie Robinson, an African American college man and former track star, joined the major-league Brooklyn Dodgers.

By then Paige was forty years old—but he was more determined than ever to stay in the game. "We don't stop playing because we get old," he said. "We get old because we stop playing." Still, he knew that age would catch up with him one day. "I'm just praying I get into the big show before my speedball loosens."

In October 1947 Paige married longtime sweetheart Lahoma Brown. She was with him the next year when he was invited to try out for the major-league Cleveland Indians.

"You can do it," Lahoma told him. "You know you can."

She was right. On July 7, 1948, Paige's forty-second birthday, he signed with the Cleveland Indians. His determination had paid off! After twenty-five years as one of baseball's best pitchers, Satchel Paige had reached the majors.

Two days later, in the middle of a game against the St. Louis
Browns, Paige had his first chance to play. The fans went wild as he
walked slowly to the pitcher's mound. Reporters and photographers
were there to capture the excitement. Flashbulbs popped. Paige was
overcome with emotion. His nerves, he later said, "were jumping

every which way." He knew he wasn't pitching just for his team but also for African Americans everywhere.

Paige didn't disappoint his team *or* his fans. In 1948 he won six games and lost only one. He had helped the Cleveland Indians reach the World Series for the first time in almost thirty years! They would play the Boston Braves.

Paige was anxious to play in the World Series, and his fans were anxious, too. They shouted, "We want Satchel! We want Satchel!" But throughout the first four games, he was kept on the bench.

Finally, in the seventh inning of the fifth game, with the Indians way behind, Paige had his chance. He would be the first African American to pitch in the World Series.

He stretched. He waited. He shook his fingers. The umpires came out three times to remind him of the rules.

Paige forced himself to forget about the thousands of cheering fans, and the many more at home sitting by their radios and listening to the game. He told himself he had a "pitching job to do."

Paige got the first batter to hit a fly ball to the outfield that was caught for an out. He threw the next batter his "real trouble ball" and got him out on a ground ball to end the inning.

After that the manager replaced Paige, who had faced only two batters but had got them both out. The Indians lost that game, but they went on to win the World Series.

When the season ended, the *Sporting News* named Paige the American League Rookie of the Year. The "rookie" award was meant

to honor Paige, but it discredited his many years in the Negro
Baseball Leagues, as though they somehow didn't count.

Still, Paige stayed in the game. He pitched in the major leagues as
late as 1965, when he was fifty-nine years old. "I like keeping busy,
keeping moving," he said. "A man rusts sitting in one spot."

Surely, Paige kept playing baseball until he was almost sixty because it had taken him so long to make his way to the majors. Once he was part of the "big show," he was reluctant to leave it.

In 1971 Satchel Paige received organized baseball's greatest honor: He was elected to the Baseball Hall of Fame in Cooperstown, New York. "Don't look back," he often said. "Something might be gaining on you." But when he accepted the honor, he talked about the past. He reminded people what they had missed by keeping African Americans out of major-league baseball for so many years. "We had a lot of Satchels," he said. "We had top pitchers."

Age finally did catch up with the great Satchel Paige, who died on June 8, 1982. He was mourned by his wife, Lahoma, their children— and by millions of Americans who loved the game of baseball.

SATCHEL PAIGE: HIGHLIGHTS OF A STAR PITCHER

1906   Born in Mobile, Alabama; July 7

1913   Gets the nickname "Satchel" while working at the train depot in Mobile

1918   Enters reform school in Mount Meigs, Alabama, for stealing rings from a toy store; July 24

1924   Makes his professional baseball debut pitching for the Mobile Tigers, a semiprofessional black team in Alabama

1926   Joins the Negro Baseball Leagues, playing for the Chattanooga Black Lookouts; May 1

1934   Marries Janet Howard; October 26 (divorced 1943)

1947   Marries his second wife, Lahoma Brown; October 12
(Together they raise her daughter from a previous marriage and the six children they later have.)

1948   Signs with the American League Cleveland Indians; July 7
Pitches in game five of the World Series against the Boston Braves; October 5

1951   Starts in his first game with the American League St. Louis Browns, against the Washington Senators; July 18

1965   Pitches three innings for the American League Kansas City Athletics, against the Boston Red Sox—his final appearance in the major leagues; September 25

1971   Inducted into the Baseball Hall of Fame in Cooperstown, New York; August 9

1982   Dies in Kansas City, Missouri; June 8

SOURCES

The sources for much of the information in this book were periodicals and newspapers of the time, including the *New York Times*, as well as more recent collective biographies and Satchel Paige's autobiography (as told by David Lipman), *Maybe I'll Pitch Forever*.